Financial Reporting

Operational level | Subject F1
CIMA official revision cards

CIMA

KAPLAN
PUBLISHING

British library
cataloguing-in-publication data

A catalogue record for this book is available from the British Library.

Published by:Kaplan Publishing UK
Unit 2 The Business Centre
Molly Millars Lane
Wokingham
Berkshire
RG41 2QZ

ISBN 978-1-78740-999-6

© Kaplan Financial Limited, 2021

Printed and bound in Great Britain.

Kaplan Publishing's learning materials are designed to help students succeed in their examinations. In certain circumstances, CIMA can make post-exam adjustment to a student's mark or grade to reflect adverse circumstances which may have disadvantaged a student's ability to take an exam or demonstrate their normal level of attainment (see CIMA's Special Consideration policy). However, it should be noted that students will not be eligible for special consideration by CIMA if preparation for or performance in a CIMA exam is affected by any failure by their tuition provider to prepare them properly for the exam for any reason including, but not limited to, staff shortages, building work or a lack of facilities etc.

Similarly, CIMA will not accept applications for special consideration on any of the following grounds:

- failure by a tuition provider to cover the whole syllabus

- failure by the student to cover the whole syllabus, for instance as a result of joining a course part way through

- failure by the student to prepare adequately for the exam, or to use the correct pre-seen material

- errors in the Kaplan Official Study Text, including sample (practice) questions or any other Kaplan content or

- errors in any other study materials (from any other tuition provider or publisher).

How to use Revision Cards

The concept

- Revision Cards are a new and different way of learning, based upon research into learning styles and effective recall.

- The cards are in full colour and have text supported by a range of images, making them far more effective for visual learners and easier to remember.

- Unlike a bound text, Revision Cards can be rearranged and reorganised to appeal to kinaesthetic learners who prefer to learn by doing.

- Being small enough to carry around means that you can take them anywhere. This gives the opportunity to keep going over what you need to learn and so helps with recall.

- The content has been reduced down to the most important areas, making it far easier to digest and identify the relationships between key topics.

- Revision Cards, however you learn, whoever you are, wherever you are.........

How to use them

Revision Cards are a pack of approximately 100 cards, slightly bigger than traditional playing cards but still very easy to carry and so convenient to use when travelling or moving around. They can be used during the tuition period or at revision.

They are broken up into 3 sections.
- An overview of the entire subject in a mind map form (orange).
- A mind map of each specific topic (blue).
- Content for each topic presented so that it is memorable (green).

Each one is a different colour, allowing you to sort them in many ways.

- Perhaps you want to get a more detailed feel for each topic, why not take all the green cards out of the pack and use those.

- You could create your own mind maps using the blue cards to explore how different topics fit together.

- And if there are some topics that you understand, take those out of the pack, leaving yourself only the ones you need to concentrate on.

There are just so many ways you can use them.

Contents

Assessment guidance

The assessment will involve 60 objective testing questions in a one and a half hour period covering all of the syllabus learning outcomes. The pass mark is 100/150.

Core areas of the syllabus

A	Regulatory Environment for Financial Reporting and Corporate Governance	10%
B	Financial statements	45%
C	Principles of taxation	20%
D	Managing Cash and working capital	25%

Quality and accuracy are of the utmost importance to us so if you spot an error in any of our products, please send an email to mykaplanreporting@kaplan.com with full details, or follow the link to the feedback form in MyKaplan.

Our Quality Co-ordinator will work with our technical team to verify the error and take action to ensure it is corrected in future editions.

Overview

financial reporting

RevisionCards

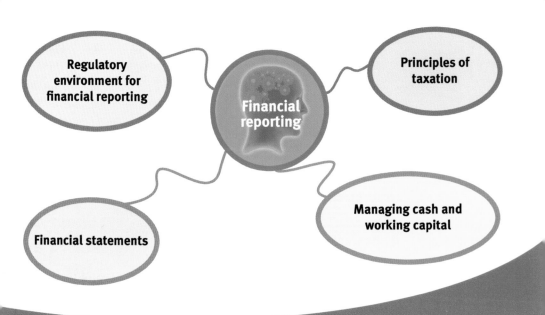

Regulatory environment for financial reporting

Principles of taxation

Financial reporting

Financial statements

Managing cash and working capital

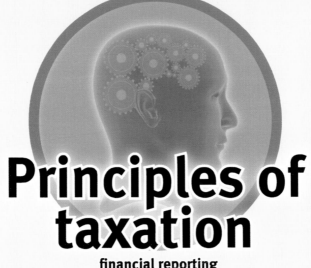

Principles of taxation

financial reporting

RevisionCards

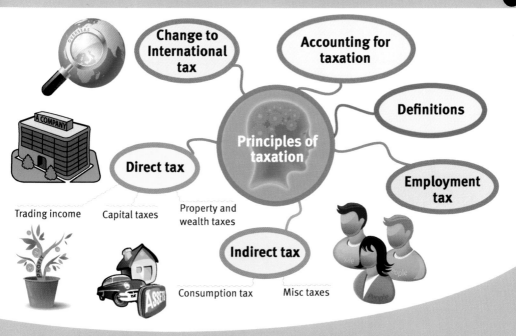

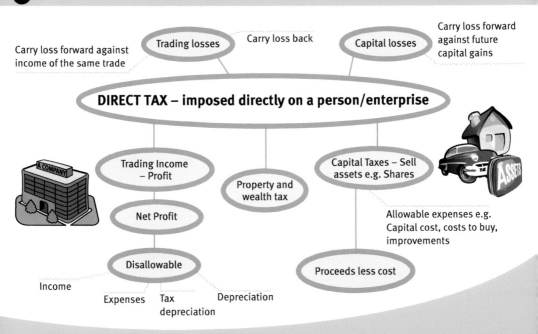

Carry loss forward against income of the same trade

Trading losses

Carry loss back

Capital losses

Carry loss forward against future capital gains

DIRECT TAX – imposed directly on a person/enterprise

Trading Income – Profit

Property and wealth tax

Capital Taxes – Sell assets e.g. Shares

Net Profit

Allowable expenses e.g. Capital cost, costs to buy, improvements

Disallowable

Proceeds less cost

Income

Expenses

Tax depreciation

Depreciation

Trading Income – Proforma

	$
Accounting profit	X
Add back: disallowable expenses	X
Less: disallowable income	(X)
Add: depreciation	X
Less: tax depreciation	(X)
Taxable profit	
X	

THIS IS A LEARN, COVER, PRACTICE PROFORMA!

The taxable profit will then be charged at the appropriate tax rate for that accounting period.

Capital Taxes – Proforma

	$
Proceeds	X
Less: costs to sell	(X)
Less: cost to buy	(X)
Less: original cost	(X)
Less: enhancements	(X)
	X
Compensation for inflation (% X cost)	(X)
Taxable gain	X

THIS IS A LEARN, COVER, PRACTICE PROFORMA!

The taxable gain will then be charged at the appropriate tax rate for that accounting period.

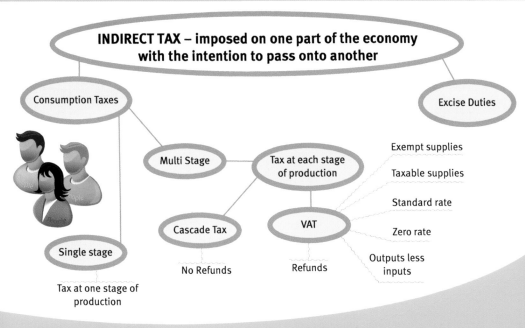

INDIRECT TAX – imposed on one part of the economy with the intention to pass onto another

Consumption Taxes

Excise Duties

Multi Stage

Tax at each stage of production

Single stage

Cascade Tax

VAT

Exempt supplies

Taxable supplies

Standard rate

Zero rate

Outputs less inputs

No Refunds

Refunds

Tax at one stage of production

Personal allowances –
amount of tax relief

PAYE – Tax deducted
at source by employer

**Employment
Tax**

Income – Salary,
bonus, benefits

Expenses – Subscriptions
to professional bodies,
occupational pension
schemes, business expenses

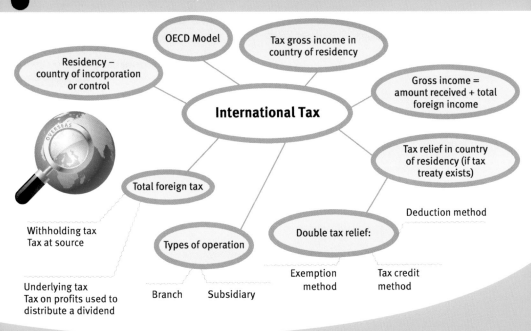

OECD Model

Tax gross income in country of residency

Residency – country of incorporation or control

Gross income = amount received + total foreign income

International Tax

Tax relief in country of residency (if tax treaty exists)

Total foreign tax

Withholding tax
Tax at source

Underlying tax
Tax on profits used to distribute a dividend

Types of operation

Branch   Subsidiary

Double tax relief:

Deduction method

Exemption method   Tax credit method

Current tax

This is the estimated amount of taxation payable on the taxable profits for the period:

	$
Accounting profit	X
Add back: disallowable expenses	X
Less: disallowable income	(X)
Add: depreciation	X
Less: tax depreciation	(X)
Taxable profit	X

THIS IS A LEARN, COVER, PRACTICE PROFORMA!

The taxable profit will then be charged at the appropriate tax rate for that accounting period.

This is recorded as:

> Dr   Income tax expense (SPL)
> Cr   Income tax liability (SOFP)

The income tax liability is always shown under current liabilities on the SOFP and the liability should always represent this year's **estimate** for taxation.

Definitions

Incidence
The incidence of a tax is the distribution of the tax burden and can be split into formal and actual incidence.

Formal incidence
This is the person who has direct contact with the tax authorities, i.e. who is legally obliged to pay the tax.

Actual incidence
This is the person who actually ends up bearing the cost of the tax.

Taxable person
The person accountable for the tax payment, e.g. Individual or company.

Competent jurisdiction
A taxable person normally pays tax in the country of origin. Competent jurisdiction is the tax authority that has the legal powers to assess and collect the taxes.

Hypothecation
This means that certain taxes are devoted entirely to certain types of expenditure, e.g. road tax is used entirely on maintaining roads.

Progressive taxes
These take an increased proportion of income as income rises.

Proportional taxes – These take the same proportion of tax as income rises.

Regressive taxes – These take a decreasing proportion of tax as income rises.

Tax consolidation – This is a type of group relief enabling trading losses to be surrendered between different companies.

Excise duties – This is a tax imposed on certain products to discourage over consumption of harmful products, to pay for extra costs (such as increased healthcare) and to tax luxuries, hence raise more revenue for the government.

Consumption taxes – This is a tax imposed on the consumption of goods and added to the purchase price.

Withholding tax – This is a tax deducted at source from foreign income.

Underlying tax – This is the tax on foreign profits that are used to distribute a dividend.

Current tax – The estimated amount of tax payable on the taxable profits of the entity for the period.

Taxable profit – This is the profit on which taxation authorites base their tax calculations.

Accounting profit – This is the profit before tax reported to the shareholders in the financial statements.

THESE ARE ALL LEARN, COVER, PRACTICE DEFINITIONS!

Regulatory environment for financial reporting

financial reporting

RevisionCards

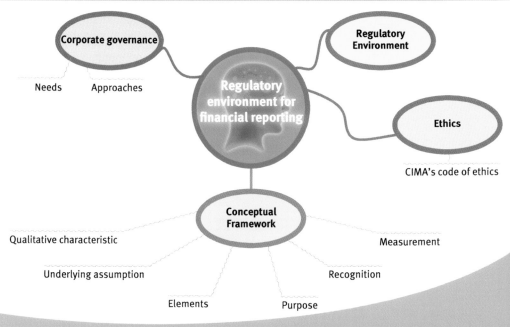

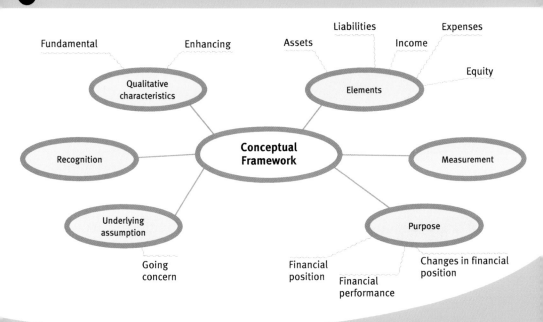

Qualitative characteristics

The Framework splits qualitative characteristics into two categories:

Fundamental qualitative characteristics

- Relevance
- Faithful representation

Enhancing qualitative characteristics

- Comparability
- Verifiability
- Timeliness
- Understandability

The elements of financial statements

Assets
An asset is a present economic resource controlled by the entity as a result of past events. An economic resource is a right that has the potential to produce economic benefits

Liability
A liability is a present obligation of the entity to transfer an economic resource as a result of past events

Equity
Equity is the residual interest in the assets of the enterprise after deducting all its liabilities.

Income
increases in assets or decreases in liabilities that result in increases in equity, other than those relating to contributions from equity participants

Expenses
Expenses are decreases in assets or increases in liabilities that result in decreases in equity, other than those relating to distributions to equity participants

YOU MUST LEARN THESE ELEMENTS!!

Recognition of the elements of financial statements

In order to recognise items in the statement of financial position or statement of profit or loss, the following criteria should be satisfied:

- It meets the definition of an element of financial statements.

- provides **relevant** information regarding the particular element

- provides a **faithful representation** of the particular element

Measurement of the elements of financial statements

Measurement is the process of determining the monetary amounts at which the elements of financial statements are to be recognised and carried in the statement of financial position and statement of profit or loss.

There are a number of different ways of measuring the elements including:

Historical cost	Current cost	Value in use	Fair value

? QUESTION – CAN YOU LINK THESE WAYS OF MEASUREMENT TO THE QUALITATIVE CHARACTERISTICS?????

Regulatory Environment

There is a need for regulation to ensure that the financial statements can be relied upon by users. Regulation promotes consistency and so helps users when interpreting statements.

Elements of regulation are:

- Local law

- Local accounting standards

- International accounting standards

- Conceptual frameworks

- Requirements of international bodies

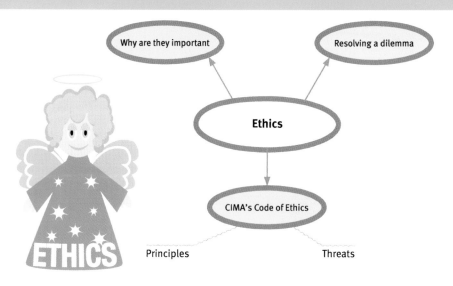

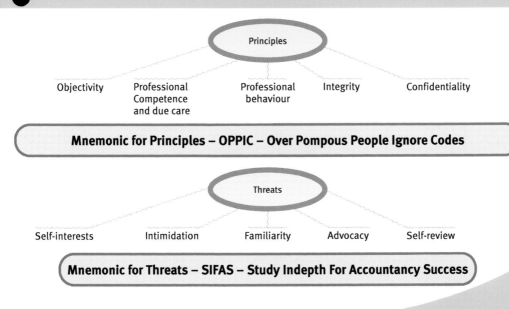

Principles

Objectivity   Professional Competence and due care   Professional behaviour   Integrity   Confidentiality

Mnemonic for Principles – OPPIC – Over Pompous People Ignore Codes

Threats

Self-interests   Intimidation   Familiarity   Advocacy   Self-review

Mnemonic for Threats – SIFAS – Study Indepth For Accountancy Success

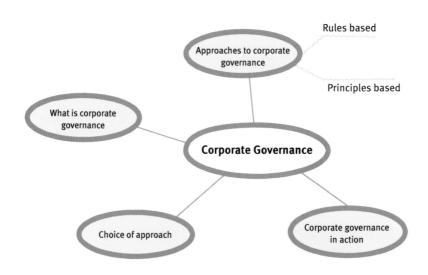

Approaches to Corporate Governance

Rules Based	Principles Based
• eg USA	• eg UK
• Applied by law	• Adhere in spirit rather than law
• Fines for not applying	• Comply or explain why

Single entity
financial statements

financial reporting

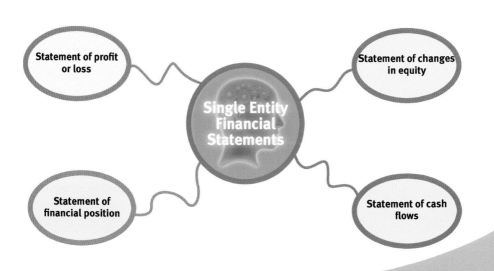

Statement of profit or loss and other comprehensive income for (Name of entity) for the year ended 31 December 20XX

Proforma:

Continuing operations:	**$**
Revenue	X
Cost of sales	(X)
Gross profitt	X
Distribution costs	(X)
Administrative expenses	(X)
Profit before interest and tax	X
Finance costs	(X)
Profit before tax	X
Tax expense	(X)
Profit for the period from continuing operations	X
Total profit for the period	X
Other comprehensive income:	
Gains/losses on revaluations	X
Total comprehensive income for the period	X

THIS IS A LEARN, COVER, PRACTICE PROFORMA!

Proformas

Statement of Changes in Equity (SOCIE) for (Name of entity) for the year ended 31 December 20XX

	Share Capital	Share Premium	Revaluation Surplus	Retained Earnings	Total
Opening balance	X	X	X	X	X
	___	___	___	___	___
Share issue	X	X		X	X
Revaluation surplus/deficit			X/(X)		X/(X)
Profit from SP&L				X	X
Dividends				(X)	(X)
Closing balance	X	X	X	X	X

Proformas

Statement of Financial Position for
(Name of entity) as at
31 December 20XX

	$	$
ASSETS		
Non-Current Assets		
Property, plant and equipment	X	
Other non-current assets	X	X
Current Assets		
Inventories	X	
Trade receivables and other receivables	X	
Cash and cash equivalents	X	X
Total assets		X

EQUITY AND LIABILITIES		
Equity		
Share capital	X	
Share premium	X	
Revaluation reserve	X	
Retained earnings	X	X
Non-current liabilities		
Long-term borrowings	X	
Long-term provisions	X	X
Current liabilities		
Trade and other payables	X	
Short-term borrowings	X	
Current tax payable	X	
Short-term provisions	X	X
Total equity and liabilities		X

Statement of cashflow for (Name of entity) for year ended 31 December 20XX

PROFORMA (Indirect method)

Cash flows from OPERATING activities	$	$
Net profit before taxation	X	
Adjustments for:		
Depreciation/amortisation/impairment	X	
Provision increases/(decreases)	X/(X)	
(Profit)/loss on disposal	(X)/X	
Interest receivable/investment income	(X)	
Finance costs	X	
Operating profit before working capital changes		X
(Increase)/decrease in inventories		(X)/X
(Increase)/decrease in receivables		(X)/X
Increase/(decrease) in payables		X/(X)
Cash generated from operations		X
Interest paid		(X)
Tax paid		(X)
Net cash from operating activities		X

Cash flows from INVESTING activities

Purchase of property, plant and equipment	(X)	
Purchase of investments	(X)	
Proceeds from sale of property, plant and equipment	X	
Investment income received	X	
Net cash from investing activities		X

Cash flows from FINANCING activities

Proceeds from share issue	X	
Proceeds /Redemption from long-term borrowings	X/(X)	
Dividends paid	(X)	
Net cash from financing activities		X
Net increase/(decrease) in cash and cash equivalents		X
Cash and cash equivalents at the beginning of the period		X
Cash and cash equivalents at the end of the period		X

THIS IS A LEARN, COVER, PRACTICE PROFORMA!

Purpose of cash flows

C ash flow is key to future survival

A ssess companies adaptability

$ olvency problems indicated early on

H ighlights where cash is generated and spent

IMPROVES THE UNDERSTANDABILITY OF THE FINANCIAL STATEMENTS

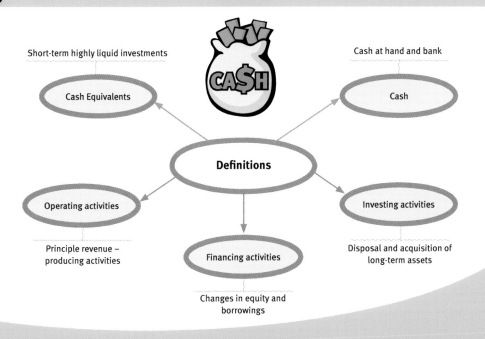

Cash is generated from operations

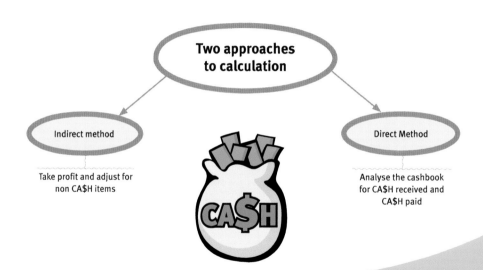

Two approaches
to calculation

Indirect method

Take profit and adjust for
non CA$H items

Direct Method

Analyse the cashbook
for CA$H received and
CA$H paid

CA$H

Proforma working of Direct method

Statement of cash flows for (Name of company) for the year ended 31 December 20XX

	$
Cash flows from operating activities	
Cash received from customers	X
Cash paid to suppliers	(X)
Cash paid to employees	(X)
Other cash payments for expenses	(X)
Cash generated from operations	X

Accounting
standards
financial reporting

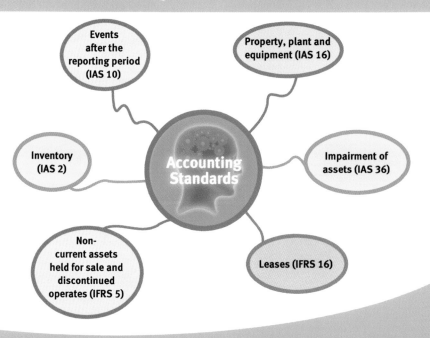

Accounting standards

The main accounting standards are covered on the following cards. For complete coverage please refer to your F1 text

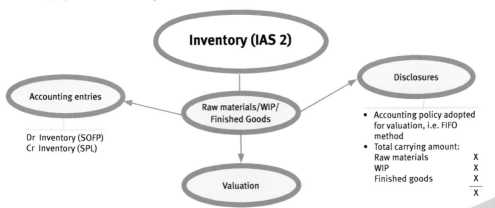

Inventory (IAS 2)

Accounting entries

Dr Inventory (SOFP)
Cr Inventory (SPL)

Raw materials/WIP/
Finished Goods

Disclosures

- Accounting policy adopted for valuation, i.e. FIFO method
- Total carrying amount:
  Raw materials   X
  WIP   X
  Finished goods   X
                       X

Valuation

IAS 2 Inventory

Inventory must be valued at lower of cost or net realisable value

Cost

Net realisable value

All costs to bring the inventory to its present location and conditions, e.g. Purchase price, transport costs, direct labour, fixed and variable overheads (fixed overheads absorbed on Normal production capacity)

Selling price less costs to sell/complete

If actual cost is variable use:

First-in, first-out (FIFO) – Value at most recent prices

Average cost (AVCO) – Value at average price

Last-in, first-out (LIFO) – Value at oldest prices Not acceptable under IAS 2

IAS 10 Events after the Reporting Period

There are two types of events:

Adjusting events – events after the reporting date which provide evidence of conditions that existed at the reporting date. These events will require an adjustment to the accounts.

Non-adjusting events – events after the reporting date which provide evidence of conditions that have arose since the reporting date. These events will not require an adjustment to the accounts but if material, disclosure should be made in the notes.

The following are the main types of adjusting and non-adjusting events:

Adjusting events	Non-adjusting events
Discovery of errors or fraud	Fluctuations in tax/exchange rates
Adjustment to valuations of inventory	Issue of shares
Major customers going into liquidation	Acquisition/disposal/merger of business
Completion of an insurance claim	Fires or floods
Completion of a court case	Plans for restructuring

Tangible assets (owned) (IAS 16)

Initial measurement

Capitalise –
Purchase price
Directly attributable costs to bring
to the location
Initial estimates of dismantling and
restoring site

Expense –
Repairs
Annual/regular costs

Capitalise –
Improvements to increase
economic benefits

Shown on Statement of financial
position (SOFP) as Property plant
and equipment (PPE)

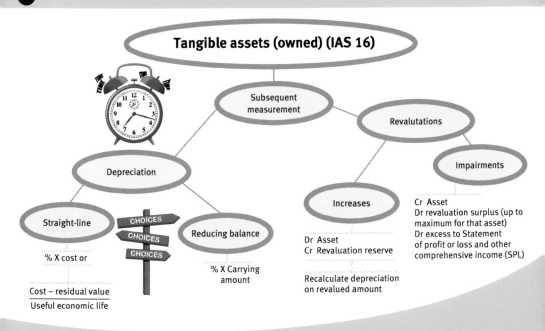

Tangible assets (owned) (IAS 16)

Subsequent measurement

Revalutations

Impairments

Cr Asset
Dr revaluation surplus (up to maximum for that asset)
Dr excess to Statement of profit or loss and other comprehensive income (SPL)

Depreciation

Increases

Dr Asset
Cr Revaluation reserve

Recalculate depreciation on revalued amount

Straight-line

CHOICES
CHOICES
CHOICES

Reducing balance

% X cost or

% X Carrying amount

Cost – residual value
Useful economic life

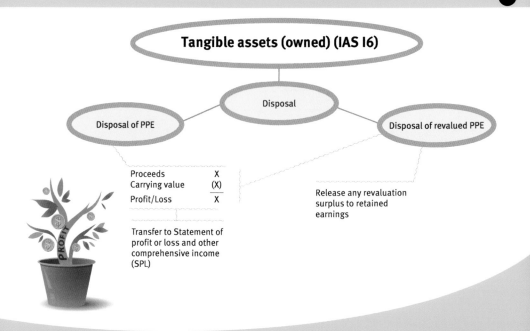

Tangible assets (owned) (IAS 16)

Disposal

Disposal of PPE

Disposal of revalued PPE

Proceeds	X
Carrying value	(X)
Profit/Loss	X

Transfer to Statement of profit or loss and other comprehensive income (SPL)

Release any revaluation surplus to retained earnings

Disclosure

Property, plant and equipment note for (Give name of entity) for the year ended 31 December 20XX

	Land & buildings $	Plant & Equipment $	Vehicles $	Total $
Cost				
At 1 January 20XX	X	X	X	X
Additions	X	X	X	X
Disposals	(X)	(X)	(X)	(X)
Revaluations	X/(X)	X/(X)	X/(X)	X/(X)
Assets held for sale	(X)	(X)	(X)	(X)
At 31 December 20XX	X	X	X	X
Depreciation				
At 1 January 20XX	X	X	X	X
Disposals	(X)	(X)	(X)	(X)
Revaluations	(X)	(X)	(X)	(X)
Assets held for sale	(X)	(X)	(X)	(X)
Charge for the year	X	X	X	X
At 31 December 20XX	X	X	X	X
Carrying amount				
At 31 December 20XX	X	X	X	X
At 1 January 20XX	X	X	X	X

IFRS 5 Discontinued Activities and Assets Held for Sale

Asset held for sale

Conditions:

- Available for immediate sale in its present condition

- The sale is highly probable

- A reasonable price has been set

- The sale is expected to be completed within a year.

If the asset meets **all** of the above criteria it will be treated as an "asset held for sale" on the statement of financial position and valued at the **lower** of it's:

Carrying value   Fair value less costs to sell

> Any impairment on valuation should be charged to the appropriate expense category on the SPL.

REMEMBER – ASSETS HELD FOR SALE ARE NO LONGER DEPRECIATED.

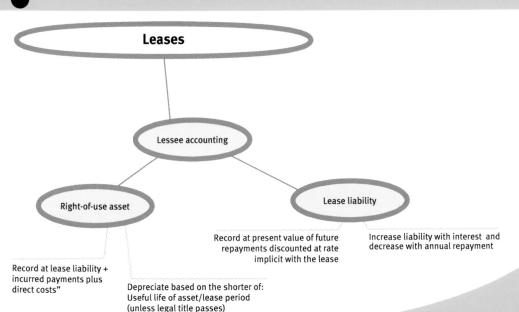

Leases

Lessee accounting

Right-of-use asset

Lease liability

Record at present value of future repayments discounted at rate implicit with the lease

Increase liability with interest and decrease with annual repayment

Record at lease liability + incurred payments plus direct costs"

Depreciate based on the shorter of: Useful life of asset/lease period (unless legal title passes)

Lessee accounting

Lease Liability – Workings

Actuarial method (payment in arrears)

Year	B/fwd	Interest %	Payment	C/fwd
1	X	X	(X)	X
2	X	X	(X)	X

Actuarial method (payment in advance)

Year	B/fwd	Payment	Sub total	Interest %	C/fwd
1	X	(X)	X	X	X
2	X	(X)	X	X	X

The interest charge column represents the charge to the Statement of profit or loss and other comprehensive income (SOPLOCI).

The balance carried forward column represents the total liability on the Statement of financial position (SFP).

Short-term finance and investments

financial reporting

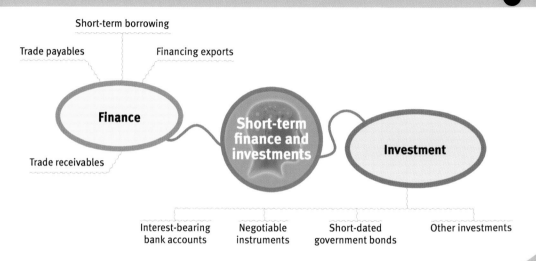

Short-term sources of finance

Trade Payables

Advantage	Disadvantage
• Easy to arrange	• Suppliers may stop supplying or increase prices

Trade receivables (factoring or invoice discounting)

Advantage	Disadvantage
• Cost saving on credit control function and factor may take reasonality for irrecoverable debts	• Expensive and customers may not be happy with the factor taking responsibility for the debt

Bank Overdraft

Advantage	Disadvantage
• Flexible and unsecured	• Expensive and repayable on demand

Financing Exports

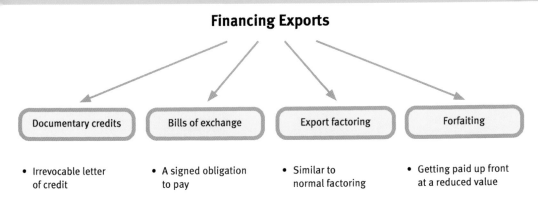

Documentary credits	Bills of exchange	Export factoring	Forfaiting
• Irrevocable letter of credit	• A signed obligation to pay	• Similar to normal factoring	• Getting paid up front at a reduced value

Short term investments

Cash surpluses can be invested in a range of short-term interest-earning investments such as:

- Interest-bearing bank accounts, e.g. bank deposit accounts, money market deposits.

- Negotiable instruments, e.g. bank notes, bearer bonds, certificates of deposit, bill of exchange, treasury bills.

- Investing in short-dated government bonds.

- Other short-term investments, e.g. corporate bonds, commercial paper.

Working capital management

financial reporting

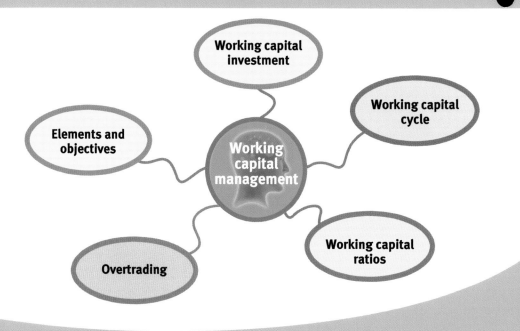

Elements and Objectives

Working capital is the excess of current assets over current liabilities

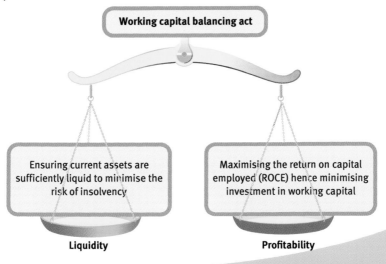

Working capital balancing act

Ensuring current assets are sufficiently liquid to minimise the risk of insolvency

Maximising the return on capital employed (ROCE) hence minimising investment in working capital

Liquidity

Profitability

Working Capital Cycle

The working Capital Cycle is the length of time between the entity's outlay on raw materials, wages and other expenditure and the inflow of cash from the sale of goods

Raw materials holding period	x
Less: payables' payment period	(x)
WIP holding period	x
Finished goods holding period	x
Receivables' collection period	x
Working Capital Cycle	x

Influences on the working capital cycle

- Working capital policies/management.

- Management efficiency.

- Industry.

- Seasonality.

- Power of buyers/suppliers.

Working Capital Ratios

Raw materials Inventory days $= \dfrac{\text{Average raw materials inventory held}}{\text{Materials usage*}} \times 365$

*Where not available use purchases

WIP Inventory days $= \dfrac{\text{Average WIP}}{\text{Production costs*}} \times 365$

*Where not available use cost of sales

Finished goods Inventory days $= \dfrac{\text{Average finished goods inventory held}}{\text{Cost of goods sold}} \times 365$

Trade receivable days $= \dfrac{\text{Average receivables}}{\text{Credit sales}} \times 365$

Trade payable days $= \dfrac{\text{Average Payables}}{\text{Credit Purchases}} \times 365$

Working capital Investment

This will depend upon:

- The industry the entity operates in.

- The type of products sold.

- Whether the products are manufactured or brought in.

- The level of sales.

- Inventory management, receivables collection and payables payment policies.

- The efficiency of management of the working capital.

Managing working capital

Three policies exist:

- An aggressive policy – This approach attempts to reduce costs by holding the lowest levels of cash, inventory, receivables and payables as possible.

- A conservative policy – This approach attempts to reduce risks by holding high levels of cash, inventory, receivables and payables. This produces a long operating cycle.

- A moderate policy – This adopts a middle ground between aggressive and conservative approaches.

Overtrading

If a business does not have access to sufficient capital to find growth in trading it is said to be overtrading

Typical indicators

- A rapid increase in turnover.

- A rapid increase in the volume of current assets.

- Most of the increase in assets being financed by credit.

- A dramatic drop in the liquidity ratios.

Working capital management – receivables and payables

financial reporting

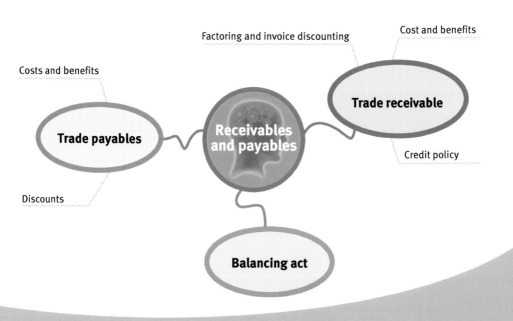

Trade Receivables

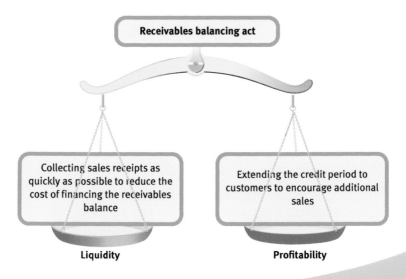

Trade Receivables

Factoring

Factoring is the outsourcing of the credit control department to a third party

Advantage	Disadvantage
• Short-term cash boost	• Expensive long-term
• Administration savings	• Customer stigma

Invoice Discounting

Invoice discounting is a method of raising finance against the security of receivables without using the receivables ledger administration services of a factor.

Advantage	Disadvantage
• Short-term cash boost	• Expensive long-term
• Customer is unaware	• Extra administration costs

Costs and Benefits – Receivables

Costs of granting credit to customers

- Exposure to irrecoverable debts

- Lost interest

- Staff costs for credit control department

- Discounts

Benefits of granting credit

- Extra sales

- Maintains customer goodwill

- Money collected more securely

Cost of financing receivables

Finance cost = receivables balance x interest (overdraft rate)

$$\text{Sales} \times \frac{\text{receivables days}}{365}$$

Trade Payables

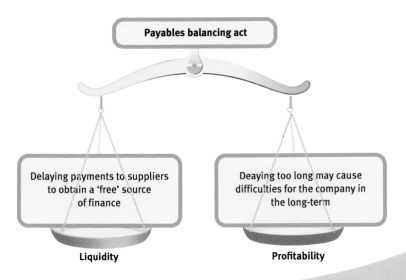

Payables balancing act

Delaying payments to suppliers to obtain a 'free' source of finance

Deaying too long may cause difficulties for the company in the long-term

Liquidity

Profitability

Costs and Benefits – Payables

Costs of taking credit from suppliers

- Loss of settlement discounts

- Loss of credit status / supplier goodwill

- Staff costs

Benefits of taking credit

- Convenient and informal cheap short term finance

The annual cost of discount

$$\text{Annual cost} = \left(1 + \frac{\text{Discount}}{\text{amount left to pay}}\right)^{\text{No of periods}} - 1$$

Working capital management – inventory control

financial reporting

RevisionCards

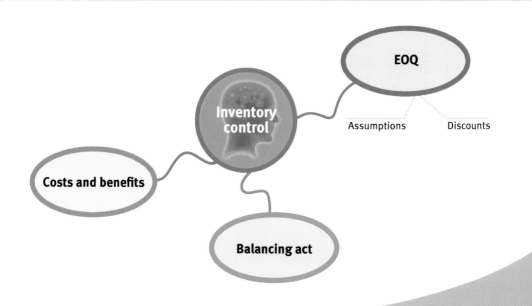

The balancing act

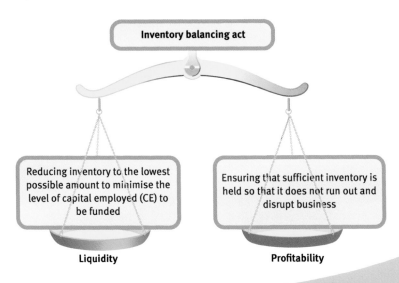

Costs of high inventory levels

- purchase costs (money tied up)

- holding costs

  - storage stores

  - administration

  - risk of theft/damage/obsolescence.

Costs of low inventory levels

- greater risk of stockouts:

  - lost contribution

  - production stoppages

  - emergency orders

- high re-order/setup costs

- lost quantity discounts.

EOQ (Economic Order Quantity)

$$EOQ = \sqrt{\frac{2C_0D}{C_H}}$$

Where:

C_0 = cost per order

D = annual demand

C_H = cost of holding one unit for one year.

A good mnemonic to remember this formula is 2 cod and chips!

EOQ Assumptions

- demand is constant and known

- lead time is constant and known

- purchase price is constant

- no buffer inventory held (not needed).

EOQ – Dealing with quantity discounts

Step 1: Calculate EOQ, ignoring discounts.

Step 2: If the EOQ is below the quantity qualifying for a discount, calculate the total annual inventory cost arising from using the EOQ.

Step 3: Recalculate total annual inventory costs using the order size required to just obtain each discount.

Step 4: Compare the cost of Steps 2 and 3 with the saving from the discount, and select the minimum cost alternative.

Step 5: Repeat for all discount levels.

Working capital management – cash control

financial reporting

RevisionCards

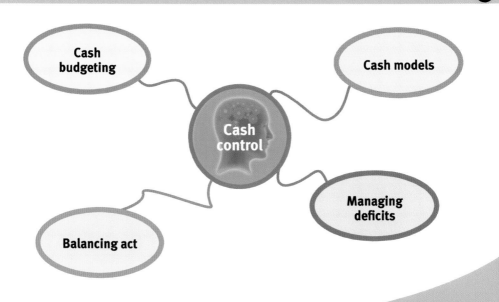

The balancing act

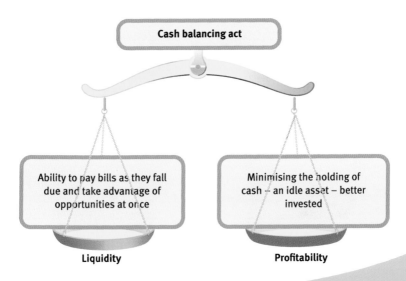

Cash needs to be readily available

Failure to carry sufficient cash will result in:

- loss of settlement discounts

- loss of suppliers goodwill

- poor industrial relations

- potential liquidation.

Cash budgeting and forecast

A **cash forecast** is an estimate of cash receipts and payments for a future period under existing conditions.

A **cash budget** is a commitment to a plan for cash receipts and payments for a future period after taking any action necessary to bring the forecast into line with the overall business plan.

Benefits of Cash Budgeting

- Can plan for deficits (see over).

- Can plan capital expenditure.

- Can be used to gain access to finance.

- Can identify working capital management issues.

- Forces management to recognize problems.

Measures to improve a forecast deficit

- additional short-term borrowing

- negotiating a higher overdraft limit with the bank

- the sale of short-term investments, if the company has any

- using different forms of financing to reduce cash flows in the short term, such as leasing instead of buying outright

- changing the amount of discretionary cash flows, deferring expenditures or bringing forward revenues.